Jesus
His Birth

Matthew 1:18-25, 2:1-16
Luke 1:26-56, 2:1-20
John 1:14

by

Rebecca Daniel

illustrated by
Nancee McClure

A Christian Education Activity Book

NOTE: The activities in this book were written using the King James Version of the Bible, so always use this version to solve the puzzles.

Cover by Nancee McClure

ISBN No. 0-86653-213-7
Printing No. 9876

GOOD APPLE, INC.
BOX 299
CARTHAGE, IL 62321-0299

INTRODUCTION

Can you imagine young Mary's awe when the angel Gabriel appeared to her? She must have been overjoyed by the news that God had chosen her to be the mother of His son. "And the angel said unto her, Fear not, Mary: for thou has found favour with God."

Mary was engaged to Joseph, a carpenter, in Nazareth. She did not tell Joseph that the angel had visited her. She went to visit her cousin Elisabeth. The angel had told Mary, "And, behold, thy cousin Elisabeth, she hath also conceived a son. . . ." The two women prayed and thanked God together. Mary sang her praise to God. "My soul doth magnify the Lord, And my spirit hath rejoiced in God my Saviour." Mary stayed with her cousin Elisabeth about three months and returned to her own house.

After returning to Nazareth, Mary told Joseph about the angel's visit. At first Joseph was confused. One night an angel appeared to him in a dream and said, "And she shall bring forth a son, and thou shalt call his name JESUS: for he shall save his people from their sins."

Joseph soon learned of some bad news. "And it came to pass in those days, that there went out a decree from Caesar Augustus, that all the world should be taxed." Mary and Joseph had to make the long journey to Bethlehem. When they arrived in Bethlehem, there were no rooms in the inn. A kind innkeeper offered his stable as a resting place for the young couple. Thankful for the shelter, they settled in for the night.

"And there were in the same country shepherds abiding in the field keeping watch over their flock by night." Suddenly a great light appeared in the sky! Angels sang, "Glory to God in the highest, and on earth peace, good will toward men." The eager shepherds, full of wonder and awe, hurried to Bethlehem to see Jesus.

In a land far to the east, wise men also noticed a strange star in the sky. They knew that the star was a sign from God and that the great King of the Jews had been born. "When they saw the star, they rejoiced with exceeding great joy." The wise men travelled for months in search of Jesus until they reached Jerusalem. They asked King Herod about the birth of the new king. King Herod lied and told the wise men to find the baby so he too could worship Him. Of course, this was part of a wicked plan to protect his own throne.

The wise men left the palace and followed the star to the house of Joseph and Mary. The wise men presented gifts of gold, frankincense, and myrrh to baby Jesus. "And being warned of God in a dream that they should not return to Herod, they departed into their own country another way."

Joseph was also warned of Herod's anger in a dream. "Arise, and take the young child and his mother, and flee into Egypt, and be thou there until I bring thee word: for Herod will seek the young child to destroy him. When he arose, he took the young child and his mother by night, and departed into Egypt."

BIRTH OF JESUS ANNOUNCED

Luke 1:26-28

To discover the secret message, write the letter of the alphabet that comes before each letter found below.

Pof ebz Nbsz xbt tjuujoh

___ ___ _____ ___ _______

bmpof. B wpjdf tbje,

________ _ ______ _____

"Epo'u cf bgsbje, Nbsz. J

_______ __ ________ ______ _

bn Hbcsjfm, uif bohfm pg

__ _________ ___ _______ ___

uif Mpse."

___ ________

Name________________________________

Read each sentence. If the statement is correct, circle the letter under the letter *T*. If the statement is not correct, circle the letter under the letter *F*. To discover the secret message, fill in the blanks with the appropriate letters.

SECRET MESSAGE:

__ __ __   __ __ __   __ __ __ __ __ __ __

1 2 3   4 5 6   7 8 9 10 11 12 13

	T	F
1. The angel's name was Gabriel.	y	c
2. The angel was sent from God.	o	e
3. The city was Nazareth.	u	a
4. The woman's name was Elisabeth.	b	a
5. The woman's husband was David.	u	r
6. The angel didn't speak.	w	e
7. The angel said, "The Lord is with you."	f	g
8. The angel said, "Blessed art thou among women."	a	s
9. The angel said, "You should marry Joseph."	w	v
10. The angel said, "Move to Galilee."	t	o
11. The angel said, "Thou art highly favoured."	r	u
12. Mary was the daughter of Joseph.	x	e
13. Joseph was of the house of David.	d	t

Can you spell four people mentioned in the Scriptures using only the letters in the box?

____

____

____

____

G	L	E
A	O	I
B	R	D
M	Y	V

Name________________________

CALL HIS NAME JESUS

Luke 1:29-33

Each row of jumbled letters found below contains a hidden word. To discover the secret message, circle the hidden words and write them in the order they are found on the blanks below.

SECRET MESSAGE: _ _ _ _

_ _ _ _ _ _   _ _ _ _ _   _   _ _ _ _

_ _ _   _ _ _ _ _   _ _ _ _

_ _ _ _   _ _ _ _ _ _ _.

P Y X T H O U E B P E Z O F F O
E X Z O S H A L T P B N O D K E
M I X E S T F H A V E M O B N N
N O P A A B E N J K L M N I E A
S O N M K I U E T Y E R F V D S
I O U Y H T A N D G H O P E E M
E R T C A L L O I U E J D H Y R
I O U Y N B H I S K E M E I N E
N A M E B H I M E U G I I F I D
T I O M E N D K E J E S U S O I

Name________________________________

"(3 down) shall be (5 down), and (7 across) be called the Son of the (2 down): and the (8 down) God shall (5 across) unto him the (1 across) of his (6 across) (4 down). . . ."

Luke 1:32

Begin in the center box. Draw a continuous line from letter to letter going left, right, up or down. You may not move diagonally. When you finish, the letters should form a sentence.

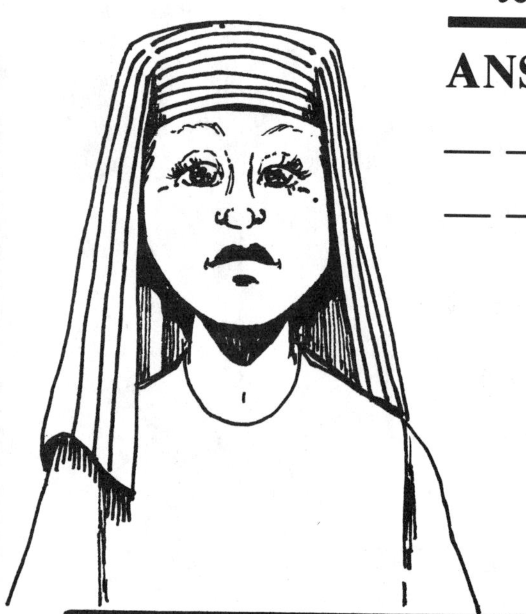

ANSWER: _ _ _ _ _ _ _ _ _ _ _ _

_ _ _ _ _ _ _ _ _ _ _ _ _ _ _

_ _ _ _.

H	A	L	L	H
S	N	E	V	A
M	O	*	H	I
O	E	N	D	S
D	G	N	I	K

Name______________________________

NOTHING SHALL BE IMPOSSIBLE

Luke 1:34-38

To discover the secret message, follow the directions carefully.

MERO WTW NYI UNWARFIENW

_____ _____ ____ ____________

HYD IHTF BYULW HEPPAN. CUI

____ ____ ______ _______ ____

FHA FETW, "T EM IHA FARVENI

____ _____ ___ ___ ____ ________

YS IHA LYRW."

___ ____ _______

Change all the A's to E's.
Change all the E's to A's.
Change all the O's to Y's.
Change all the Y's to O's.
Change all the D's to W's.
Change all the W's to D's.
Change all the C's to B's.
Change all the B's to C's.
Change all the F's to S's.
Change all the S's to F's.
Change all the T's to I's.
Change all the I's to T's.
The other letters are correct.

Name______________________________

To discover the secret message, write every other letter moving clockwise around the circle. You must decide where to begin.

SECRET MESSAGE: _ _ _ _ _

_ _ _   _ _ _ _ _ _ _ _ _ _   _ _ _ _ _ _ _

_ _   _ _ _ _ _ _ _ _ _ _ _ _ _ _ _.

E H W A I L T L H B G E O I D M N P O O T S H S I I N B G L S

Make up your own circle puzzle using the Scriptures.

What word found in Luke 1:34-38 can you put in the middle that makes three-letter words of the letters going down?

f	e	s	a	a	t	s	a	b	o
r	e	t	e	k	e	d	d	w	l

Name______________________________________

MARY VISITS ELISABETH

Luke 1:39-45

Use the number code to solve this puzzle.

A=1, B=2, C=3, D=4, E=5, F=6, G= 7, H=8, I=9, J=10, K=11, L=12, M=13, N=14, O=15, P=16, Q=17, R=18, S=19, T=20, U=21, V=22, W=23, X=24, Y=25, Z=26

13,1,18,25 23,5,14,20 20,15 19,5,5

_______ _______ ____ ____

8,5,18 3,15,21,19,9,14 5,12,9,19,1,2,5,20,8.

____ _______ __________

5,12,9,19,1,2,5,20,8 23,1,19 7,15,9,14,7

__________ _____ _______

20,15 8,1,22,5 1 19,15,14, 1,12,19,15.

____ _____ _ _____ ______

20,8,5 23,15,13,5,14 16,18,1,25,5,4

____ _______ _______

20,15,7,5,20,8,5,18 1,14,4 20,8,1,14,11,5,4

__________ ____ _________

7,15,4.

_____

Name________________________________

Finish these magic word squares by spelling words found in the Scriptures. The words must read down as well as across.

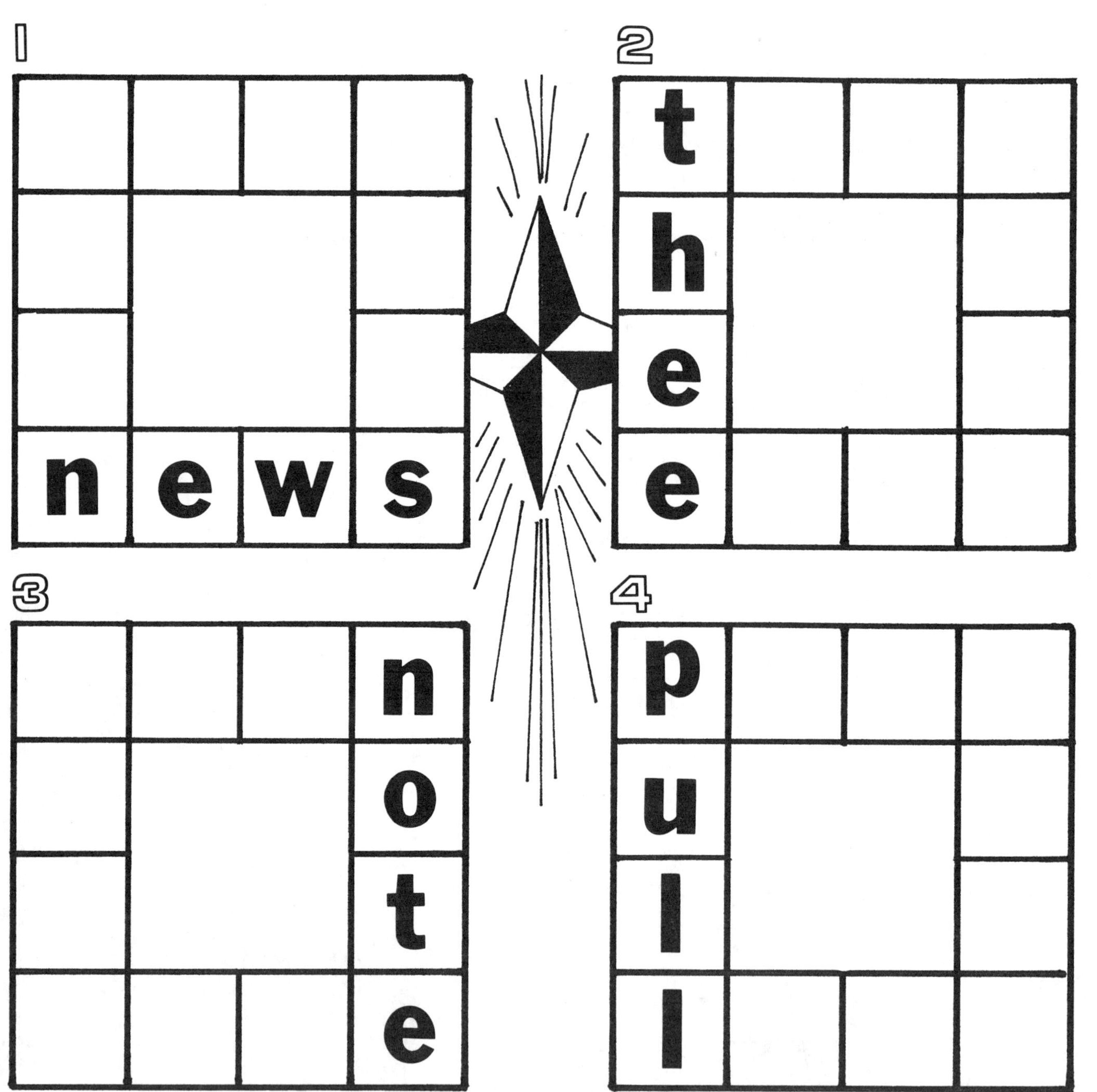

Make up your own magic word squares using words found in the Scriptures.

Name____________________________________

MARY'S HYMN OF PRAISE

Luke 1:46-56

Complete each word by adding one letter. The words are all found in the Scriptures. Then read down to discover the secret message.

ANSWER: _ _ _ _ _ _ _ _ _ _ _ _ _ _ _ _ _.

__ath
beh__ld
__ow
merc__

sp__rit
ble__sed

t__ings
__s
__trength

ow__
ex__lted
i__agination
s__nt

Name____

Begin in the upper left-hand corner and end in the lower right-hand corner. Find a path through the letters that spells a message. You must move across or down. You may not move diagonally.

M	Y	S	S	M	O	U	M	M	M	M
Y	S	O	O	Y	S	L	Y	Y	Y	Y
O	U	U	L	U	L	D	S	O	S	S
S	O	L	D	O	T	O	O	S	U	O
U	L	D	O	T	H	T	L	U	O	U
M	Y	O	T	H	M	H	U	L	L	O
S	O	T	H	M	A	G	D	D	D	D
U	L	H	S	A	G	N	I	O	T	O
D	O	S	A	G	N	I	F	Y	H	T
S	A	T	I	S	F	M	Y	T	M	A
D	O	T	H	M	A	Y	T	H	L	O
G	N	I	F	Y	T	H	H	E	L	R
M	J	L	O	R	D	M	I	E	O	O
D	O	T	H	M	A	G	N	I	R	D

The puzzle below has two words scrambled together. Use the clues to discover both words.

Remove the lady and the Lord is left.

A A S M V U R I O Y R

The lady is __ __ __ __.
Another name for the Lord is

__ __ __ __ __ __ __.

Name____

TO BE TAXED

Luke 2:1-5; Matthew 1:18-25

Add the correct vowels and put spaces between the words to discover the secret message.

SECRET MESSAGE: _ _ _ _ _ _ _

_ _ _ _ _ _ _ _ _ _ _ _ _ _

_ _ _ _ _ _ _ _ _ _ _ _ _ _ _ _ _

_ _ _ _ _ _ _ _ _ _ _ _ _ _ _ _ _ _ _

_ _ _ _ _ _ _. _ _ _ _ _ _ _ _ _ _ _

_ _ _ _ _ _ _ _ _ _ _ _ _. _ _ _

_ _ _ _ _ _ _ _ _ _ _ _ _ _

_ _ _ _ _ _ _ _ _ _ _ _ _ _ _ _ _ _ _.

J S P H N D M R Y W N T F R M G L L
T B T H L H M T B T X D .
M R Y R D N D N K Y .
T W S T M F R J S S T B B R N .

Name____

Find the shortest path through the maze. Color the path. Write the letters in the order they are found to discover the secret message.

SECRET MESSAGE: _ _ _ _ _ _

_ _ _ _ _   _ _ _ _ _ _ _

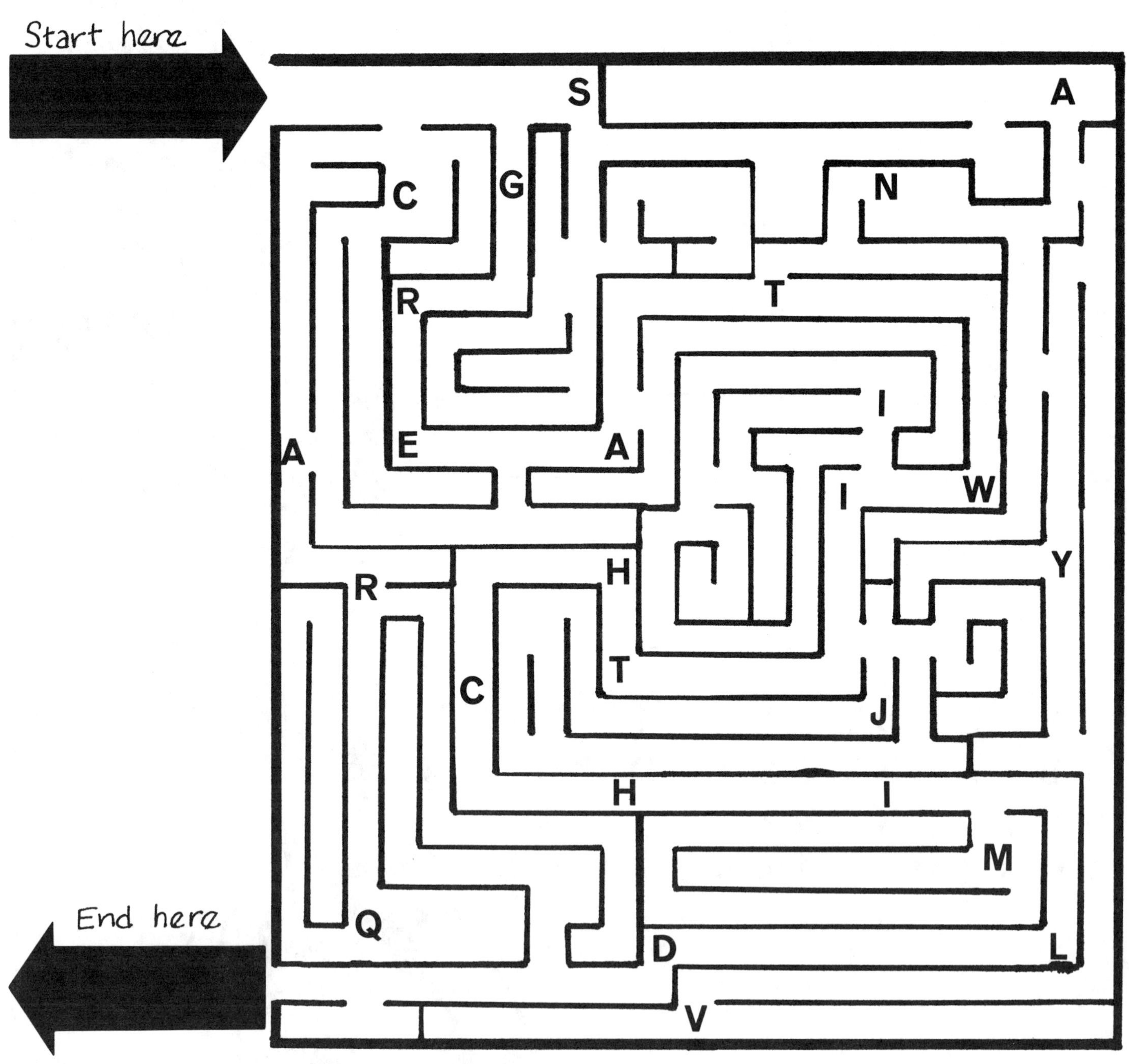

Name____

JESUS IS BORN

Luke 2:6, 7; John 1:14

Cross out one letter in each word below to spell the secret message. Then write your own message and put one extra letter in each word. Ask a friend to solve your puzzle.

"HAND SHED BROUGHTS FOURTH

_______ _______ _______ _______

HERE FIRSTBORNE SOON, HAND

_______ _______ _______ _______

SWRAPPED SHIM INN

_______ _______ _______

SWADDLINGE RCLOTHES, SAND

_______ _______ _______

SLAID SHIM TIN AM MANGERS."

_______ _______ _______ _______ _______

Name_______________________________

Unscramble the words below, and then unscramble the sentence to discover the secret message.

SECRET MESSAGE:

"_ _ _ _ _ _ _ _ _ _ _ _ _ _ _ _

_ _ _ _ _ _ _ _ _ _ _ _ _ _ _

_ _ _ _ _ _ _ _ _ _ _ _ _ _ _"

METH SAW NIN ROF
ERHTE MORO HTE NI
ON SUEBCAE

Fill in the blanks to spell words found in Luke 2:6,7 and John 1:14.

_ o
o _
_ o _
_ o _ _
_ _ o _ _
_ o _ _ _
_ _ o _ _ _ _

_ o
_ o _
_ oo _
_ _ o _ _
o _ _ _
_ _ o _ _ _
_ _ _ o _ _ _ _

Name____

ANGELS SING

Luke 2:8-14

To discover the secret message, follow the directions carefully.

SECRET MESSAGE: "__ __   __ __ __ __ __ __ __

__ __ __ __ __   __ __ __ __   __ __ __ __ __

__ __ __ __ __ __ __ __ __ __ __   __ __ __

__ __ __ __ __ __ __ __ __ __ __ __ __

__ __ __ __ __ __ __ __ __ __,   __ __ __ __ __ __ __ __   __ __

__   __ __ __ __ __ __ __ __ __."

Cross out all the Z's in the puzzle.
Cross out the number words in lines 1,2,3,4 and 8.
Cross out the animals in lines 5,6 and 8.
Cross out the first letter in lines 1,6 and 8.
Cross out the last letter in lines 1,2,4 and 5.
Cross out the color words in lines 2,3,6 and 7.
Circle the words that are left to discover the secret message.

1.	**P**	**Z**	**Y**	**E**	**Z**	**T**	**W**	**O**	**S**	**H**	**A**	**L**	**L**	**B**
2.	**P**	**U**	**R**	**P**	**L**	**E**	**F**	**I**	**N**	**D**	**S**	**I**	**X**	**D**
3.	**R**	**E**	**D**	**T**	**H**	**E**	**F**	**I**	**V**	**E**	**B**	**A**	**B**	**E**
4.	**W**	**R**	**A**	**P**	**P**	**E**	**D**	**T**	**E**	**N**	**I**	**N**	**Z**	**A**
5.	**C**	**O**	**L**	**T**	**S**	**W**	**A**	**D**	**D**	**L**	**I**	**N**	**G**	**T**
6.	**B**	**C**	**L**	**O**	**T**	**H**	**E**	**S**	**R**	**E**	**D**	**H**	**E**	**N**
7.	**G**	**R**	**E**	**E**	**N**	**L**	**Y**	**I**	**N**	**G**	**Z**	**Z**	**I**	**N**
8.	**T**	**A**	**O**	**X**	**M**	**A**	**N**	**G**	**E**	**R**	**F**	**O**	**U**	**R**

Name______________________________

To discover the secret words, you will need your crayons. Color the spaces with one dot PURPLE. Color the spaces with two dots PINK.

Name________________________________

SHEPHERDS IN THE FIELDS

Luke 2:15-20

Use the code to solve this puzzle.

E	U	L
A	T	S
H	O	N

G	D	B
W	I	X
C	M	P

Name______________________________

Find and circle every word from the Scriptures hidden in the letter maze below. The words may be written down, across or diagonally.

"And they came with haste, and found Mary, and Joseph, and the babe lying in a manger."

Luke 2:16

H	M	A	R	W	J	O	I	L
A	N	D	J	I	I	S	N	L
S	M	A	R	O	O	T	E	Y
T	H	E	Y	Y	S	H	H	I
E	C	A	M	E	H	E	P	N
T	M	N	F	A	N	D	P	G
H	A	D	O	A	R	M	B	H
E	N	M	U	N	A	Y	A	E
B	G	A	N	D	S	N	B	H
E	E	N	D	B	A	P	E	T
M	R	G	E	R	O	N	F	A

Two letters in this message have been replaced with the letter *X*. Can you decode this message by filling in the correct letters?

MARY KEPX XHXSX XHINGS IN

______ ______ ______ ______ __

HXR HXARX.

____ ________

Name________________________________

KING HEROD

Matthew 2:1-4

To discover the secret message, follow each line and write the letters in the order they are found.

SECRET MESSAGE: __ __

__ __ __ __ __ __ __ __ __ __ __ __ __ __

__ __ __ __ __.

Name________________________________

All the vowels in the message below are incorrect. Replace the incorrect vowels with the correct vowels, and you will discover the secret message.

WHIN KENG HORID HAORD

______ ______ _______ ________

EBEOT THA WOSU MAN CAMENG

_______ _____ ______ _____ _________

TE WERSHEP THA KONG IF THA

___ __________ _____ ______ __ _____

JOWS, HA WES TRIEBLAD. HO

______ ___ _____ ___________ ___

DIMENDAD THAY TALL HOM

____________ ______ ______ _____

WHORI JASES SHIELD BU BERN.

_______ ______ ________ ___ _______

The designs below are actually words. Find the hidden letters in each design to form words which will solve this puzzle.

ANSWER: _ _ _ _ _ _ _ _ _ _ _ _ _ _ _ _ _

Name____

SAW THE STAR

Matthew 2:5-10

Can you read this rebus message? Let the Scriptures help you. Then write your own rebus message about this story.

Name______________________________

To discover the secret message, use the consonants listed below and complete the words. Cross out each letter when you have used it.

BBBDDDFGHHHHHHKKLLMNNNRRRSSTTTTWWY

__i__ __ __e__o__ __a__

a__ __ai__ __ __e __a__ __ i__

__e__ __ __e__e__ __ou__ __ __a__e

__i__ __ __ __o__e.

C C D D D F G H H H H H L L M N N R R S S T T T T W

__e __o__ __ __ __e __i__e __e__

__o __o a__ __ __ea__ __ __

__o__ __ __e __ __i__ __.

Begin in the lower right-hand box. Draw a continuous line from letter to letter going left, right, up or down. You may not move diagonally. When you finish, the letters should form a sentence.

ANSWER: __.

I	H	C	E	S
L	D	E	A	O
R	T	H	R	G
O	F	H	C	*

Name______________________________________

WISE MEN COME

Matthew 2:11,12

Read these statements about the wise men. Color the T's after the sentence if the statement is true. Color the F's after the sentence if the statement is false. The T's and F's will make letters. Fill in the blanks with the appropriate letters to discover the secret word.

SECRET WORD:

___	___	___	___	___	___	___	___	___	___
1	2	3	4	5	6	7	8	9	10

1. They found the young child.	TFFFT TFFFT TFTFT TTFTT TFFFT
2. They fell and worshipped Him.	TTTTT TFFFT TFFFT TFFFT TTTTT
3. They gave Him gifts.	TTTTF TFFTF TTTTF TFTFF TFFTF
4. They had a dream.	TTTTT TFFFF TTTTT FFFFT TTTTT
5. God told them to go to the king.	FTTTF FTTTF FFFFF FTTTF FTTTF
6. They did not return to the king.	FTTTF FFTFF FFTFF FFTFF FTTTF
7. The babe was with Mary.	TTTTF TFFTF TTTTF TFFFF TFFFF
8. Joseph was in the field working.	FFFFT FTTFT FFFFT FTTTT FTTTT
9. The baby was in the manger.	FFFFT FTTTT FFFTT FTTTT FFFFT
10. They departed into their own country.	TTTFF TFFTF TFFFT TFFFT TFFTF TTTFF

Name_______________________________________

Let the Scriptures help you solve this puzzle. Fill in the blanks with the correct words. Then place these words in the puzzle.

"AND BEING _ _ _ _ _ _ _ _ _ OF _ _ _ _ IN A _ _ _ _ _ _ _ _ _ _ _ _ THEY SHOULD NOT _ _ _ _ _ _ _ _ TO HEROD, THEY _ _ _ _ _ _ _ _ _ _ _ INTO THEIR _ _ _ COUNTRY ANOTHER _ _ _ _."

Matthew 2:12

Below are three words from the Scriptures. They have been scrambled together. Can you unscramble these three words?

M D L N C H I S F R R R A N E N G K E O Y

ANSWER: _ _ _ _ _,

_ _ _ _ _ _ _ _ _ _ _ _ _ _ _ _ **AND**

_ _ _ _ _ _

Name______________________________

FLIGHT TO EGYPT

Matthew 2:13-16

Complete these word stars by spelling words found in the Scriptures. In each star, the words always have the same middle letter.

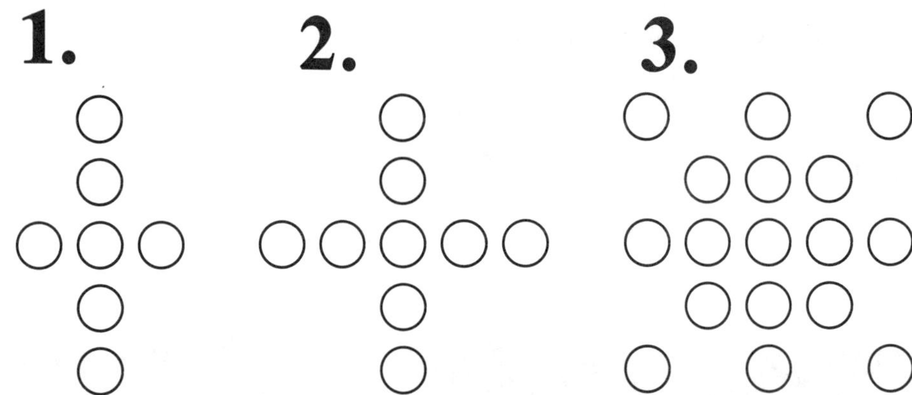

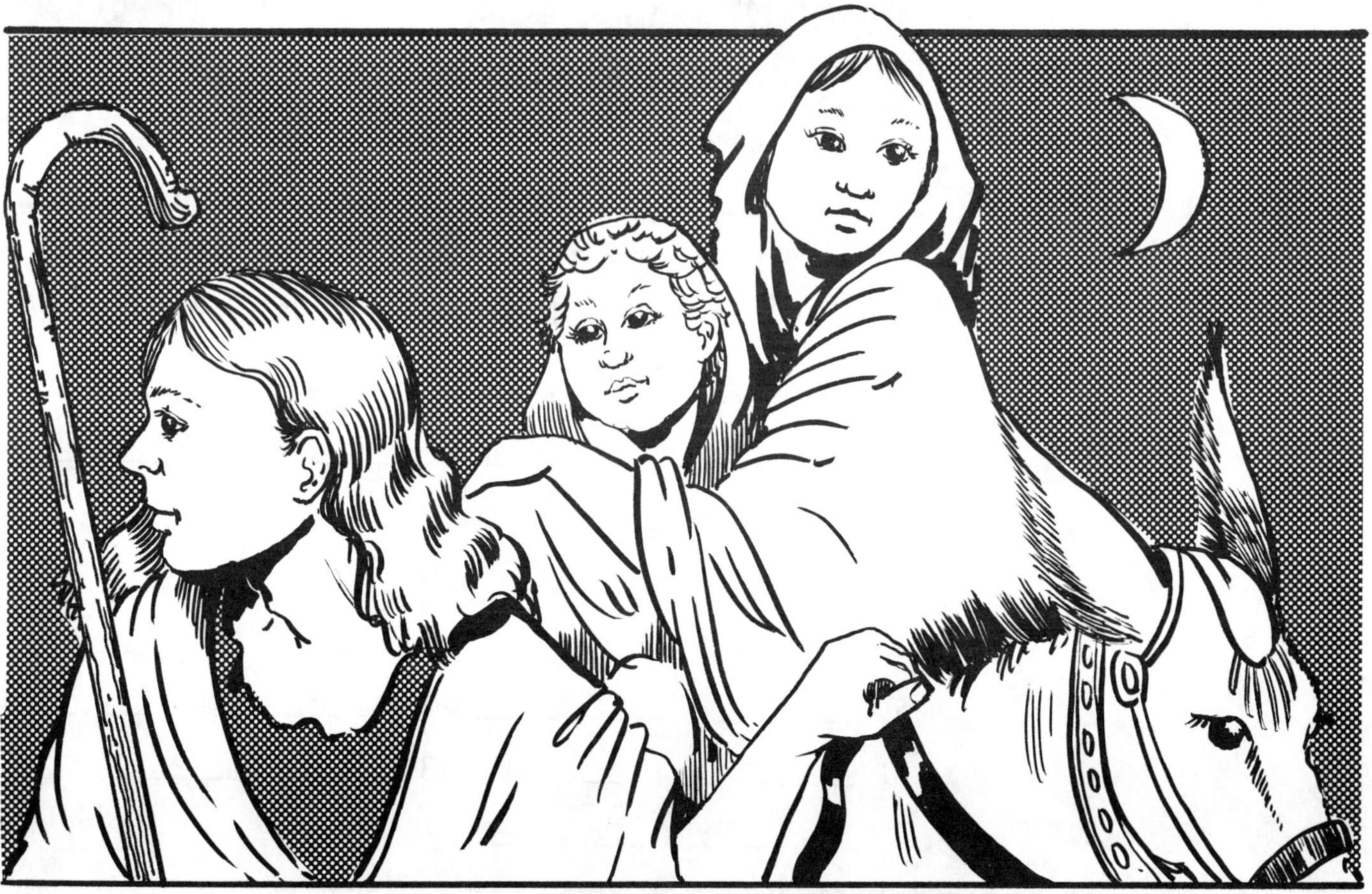

Name____

Decode the secret message. Some of the letters have been replaced with numbers. You must decide which letters stand for which numbers.

P = __ D = __ E = __ S = __ H = __ T = __ A = __

4,5,6, LORD 2,7,7,6,2,R,6,1 4,0 JO3,6,7,5 IN

_____ Lord _________r____ __o Jo_________in

2 1,R,6,2,M 2,N,1 4,OL,1 5,IM 4,0 4,2,k,6

_ __r_____m __n__ __ol__ __im __o ____k__

J,6,3,U,3 2,N,1 M,2RY 4,0 6,GY,7,4.

J_____u__ __n__ M__ry __o __gy____.

Can you find 13 words in Matthew 2:13-16 that have homonyms? Write each word and list its homonym.

1. __________ __________
2. __________ __________
3. __________ __________
4. __________ __________
5. __________ __________
6. __________ __________
7. __________ __________
8. __________ __________
9. __________ __________
10. __________ __________
11. __________ __________
12. __________ __________
13. __________ __________

Name____________________________________

REVIEW

Matthew 2:1-16

Start in any circle and move along circles that are connected by a line. How many words found in Matthew 2:1-16 can you spell? There are at least 21.

Name

PRE AND POST-TEST

If the statement is true, color the appropriately numbered spaces RED. If the statement is false, color the appropriately numbered spaces YELLOW.

1. Gabriel was the name of the angel that visited Mary.
2. Mary went to visit her cousin Elisabeth for three days.
3. Elisabeth was going to have a son, also.
4. Joseph and Mary went to Jerusalem to be taxed.
5. Jesus was born in Egypt.
6. The shepherds saw angels singing in the sky.
7. The angels told the shepherds where to find the new King.
8. The wise men followed the star and found baby Jesus lying in the manger.
9. King Herod was happy because Jesus was born.
10. The wise men brought presents to Jesus.
11. The wise men told the king where he could find baby Jesus.
12. Joseph took Mary and Jesus back to Galilee.

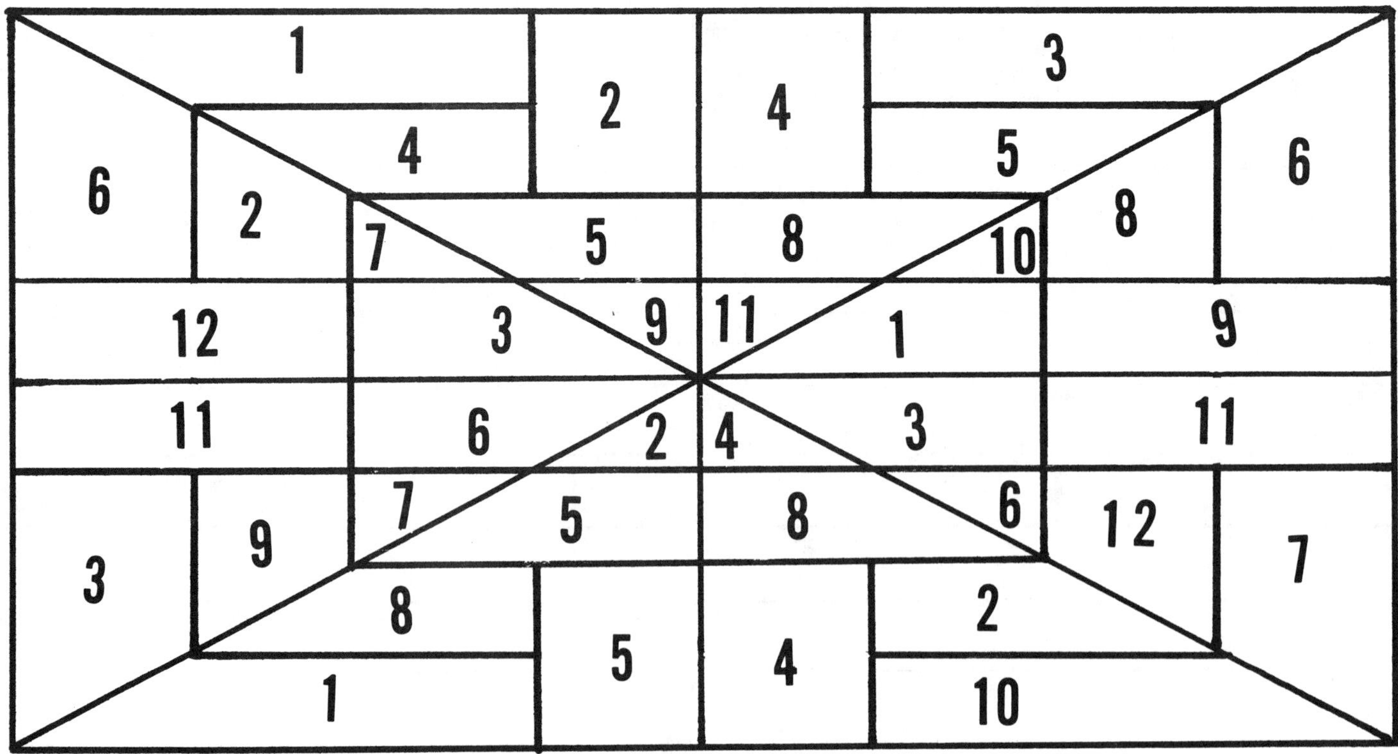

Name________________________

ANSWER KEY

3. One day Mary was sitting alone. A voice said, "Don't be afraid, Mary. I am Gabriel, the angel of the Lord."

4. You are favored. 1.t, 2.t, 3.t, 4.f, 5.f, 6.f, 7.t, 8.t, 9.f, 10.f, 11.t, 12.f, 13.t

God, Gabriel, Mary, David

5. Thou shalt have a son and call His name Jesus.

6. Across:
1. throne
5. give
6. father
7. shall

Down:
2. Highest
3. He
4. David
5. great
8. Lord

His kingdom shall have no end.

7. Mary did not understand how this could happen. But she said, "I am the servant of the Lord."

8. With God nothing shall be impossible.
overshadow

9. Mary went to see her cousin Elisabeth. Elisabeth was going to have a son also. The women prayed together and thanked God.

10. s a i d   t h a t
o   a   h   h
o   y   e   i
n e w s   e a r s
w h e n   p a s s
o   o   u   a
m   t   l   i
b a b e   l o u d

11. Holy is His name.

12. My soul doth magnify the Lord.

M Y S S M O U M M M M
Y S O O Y S L Y Y Y Y
O U U L U L D S O S S
S O L D O T O O S U O
U L D O T H T L U O U
M Y O T H M H U L L O
S O T H M A G D D D D
U L H S A G N I O T O
D O S A G N I F Y H T
S A T I S F M Y T M A
D O T H M A Y T H L O
G N I F Y T H H E L R
M J L O R D M I E O O
D O T H M A G N I R D

Mary, Saviour

13. Joseph and Mary went from Galilee to Bethlehem to be taxed. Mary rode on a donkey. It was time for Jesus to be born.

14. Great with child

15 "And she brought forth her firstborn son, and wrapped him in swaddling clothes, and laid him in a manger."

16. "because there was no room for them in the inn"
no, so, of, son, for, room, Word,
among, glory, only, forth,
should, brought, begotten

17. "Ye shall find the babe wrapped in swaddling clothes, lying in a manger."

18. Great Joy

19. Let us go unto Bethlehem and see this thing which is come to pass.

20.

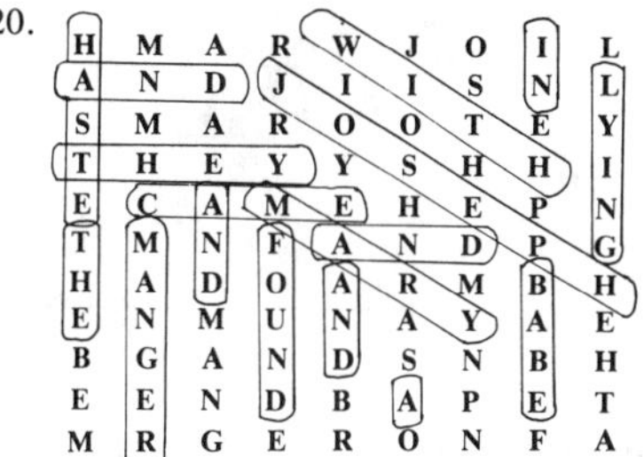

Mary kept these things in her heart.

21. We have seen His star.

22. When King Herod heard about the wise men coming to worship the King of the Jews, he was troubled. He demanded they tell him where Jesus should be born.

King of the Jews

23. "When they saw the star, they rejoiced with exceeding great joy."

24. King Herod was afraid the baby in Bethlehem would take his throne.
He told the wise men to go and search for the child.
Go search for the child.

25. WORSHIPPED
1.t, 2.t, 3.t, 4.t, 5.f, 6.t, 7.t, 8.f, 9.f, 10.t

26. "And being warned of God in a dream that they should not return to Herod, they departed into their own country another way."
gold, frankincense and myrrh

27.
1. out & young; or death & was; or arose & son
2. dream & there; or angel & might
3. arise, child, bring, which

28. The Lord appeared to Joseph in a dream and told him to take Jesus and Mary to Egypt.
P=7, D=1, E=6, S=3, H=5, T=4, A=2
to, two, too
in, inn
flee, flea
be, bee
there, their
I, eye
for, four
him, hymn
by, buy
night, knight
son, sun
sent, cent, scent
all, awl
forth, fourth
slew, slue, slough
prophet, profit

29. he, God, Jesus, was, in, Herod, king, great, star, all , east, men, wise, child, fell, gifts, go, gold, myrrh, frankincense, these

30. true: 1,3,6,7,10
false: 2,4,5,8,9,11,12

AWARD CERTIFICATE

This is to certify that

____

has successfully completed a study of the birth of Jesus. The Scriptures covered Matthew 1:18-25, 2:1-16; Luke 1:26-56, 2:1-20; John 1:14.

____

signature (teacher)

____

signature (pastor)

____

date